Betroth

COVENANTED, UNBREAKABLE, AND
EVERLASTING LOVE

Leslie J. Drummond

TRILOGY CHRISTIAN PUBLISHERS
Tustin, CA

Trilogy Christian Publishers
A Wholly Owned Subsidiary of Trinity Broadcasting Network
2442 Michelle Drive
Tustin, CA 92780

Betroth

Copyright © 2023 by Leslie J. Drummond

All Scripture quotations, unless otherwise noted, are taken from the New King James Version®. Copyright © 1982 by Thomas Nelson. Used by permission. All rights reserved.

Scripture quotations marked AMP are taken from the Amplified® Bible (AMP), Copyright © 2015 by The Lockman Foundation. Used by permission. www.Lockman.org.

All rights reserved, including the right to reproduce this book or portions thereof in any form whatsoever.

For information, address Trilogy Christian Publishing

Rights Department, 2442 Michelle Drive, Tustin, CA 92780.

Trilogy Christian Publishing/TBN and colophon are trademarks of Trinity Broadcasting Network.

For information about special discounts for bulk purchases, please contact Trilogy Christian Publishing.

Manufactured in the United States of America

Trilogy Disclaimer: The views and content expressed in this book are those of the author and may not necessarily reflect the views and doctrine of Trilogy Christian Publishing or the Trinity Broadcasting Network.

10 9 8 7 6 5 4 3 2 1

Library of Congress Cataloging-in-Publication Data is available.

ISBN 979-8-89041-230-0

ISBN (ebook) 979-8-89041-231-7 (ebook)

Contents

Dedication v
Acknowledgments vi
Foreword vii
1. Scripture of Focus 1
2. Praying God's Words of Betrothal 2
3. Poems of the Betrothed 4
    The Groom 4
    Bride and Groom 5
    And There Was Love 6
    I'm Yours Forever 6
    Loving You 7
    Will You Love Me Tomorrow? 8
    Indeed, I'll Love You Forever 8
    How I'll Love You 9
4. Selection of Prayers Adapted to God's Word 11
    Praying for Children and Parenting 11
    Praying God's Word for Deliverance 12
    Praying God's Word on Faith 14
    Praying God's Word on Faithfulness 15
    Praying God's Word on Forgiveness 16

Praying God's Word on Grace................................ 17

Praying God's Word for Health and Healing......... 19

Praying God's Word on Hope 20

Praying God's Word for Justice 21

Praying God's Word on Love 22

A Woman's Prayer for Marriage in Christ Jesus 24

Praying God's Word on Mercy 26

A Prayer for Our Pastors 27

Praying God's Word on Patience 29

Praying God's Word on Peace 31

Praying God's Word on Provision......................32

Praying God's Word for Strength 33

Praying God's Word on Thanksgiving 34

Praying God's Word on Truth............................ 35

Praying God's Word for Unity 36

Prayer of Praise and Thanksgiving for the Word of God...38

5. Scripture References by Prayer 40

6. What the Bible Says about God's Word................45

7. A Brief Commentary on Praying God's Word 50

8. Prayer for Salvation 58

Afterword 60

Dedication

This book is dedicated to the memory of my dearly departed sister, Dr. Starlene Johnson Taylor, whose encouragement, from my earliest years, has kept me moving from one achievement in life to another.

Acknowledgments

Special thanks are extended first to God our Heavenly Father, who allowed me to hold the pen for these poems and prayers. Then to my darling husband, Dr. Landson Drummond, who encouraged and sustained me throughout the writing process, I say, "Thank you for your unfailing support." Many thanks are extended to Rev. Peggie J. Carney who introduced me to praying the Word of God, and also to relatives and friends who walked with me on this journey. Further, to the publishers, editors, and staff members who took part in bringing forth Betroth, I say, "Thank you for your very important part in doing God's work." Lastly, to the readers who dared to pick up this book, I say thank you and may you be inspired to seek a close personal relationship with God through spending time in His presence and praying His Word.

Foreword

This book is written to encourage, inspire, and excite the reader to become better acquainted with God through His Word. It is commonly accepted that God talks to us through His Word—the Holy Bible. According to John 4:13, His Word is "a fountain of water springing up into everlasting life." Jesus said in John 6:63, "These words I speak are spirit and life." Open your Bible and read about the life that God has for you. You will come to know such things as a) His Word is active and powerful (see Hebrews 4:12); b) His Word heals and delivers us from our destructions (see Psalm 107:20); c) When God's Word goes out, it does not return to Him without accomplishing what He pleases...(see Isaiah 55:11); and d) God is not man that He should lie; if He says it, He will do it (see Numbers 23:19). To enhance your understanding of God's Word adapted in prayer, I have included a separate list of Scripture references for each prayer. As you read, study, and meditate on God's Word, you should begin to develop a personal relationship with Him. Hopefully, you will discover that you actually have a genuine hunger and thirst for His Word on a daily basis, and one day you may begin to pray God's Word. Note: The prayers written in this book are submitted only as examples of how to pray God's Word. Please, pray the words of God that are in your heart and mind and that address your life issues and concerns.

1

Scripture of Focus

(Hosea 2:19-20)

*"I will betroth you to Me forever;
Yes, I will betroth you to Me
In righteousness and justice,
In lovingkindness and mercy;
I will betroth you to Me in faithfulness,
And you will know the Lord."*

2

Praying God's Word of the Betrothed

Heavenly Father, thank You for betrothing me unto Yourself in righteousness and justice, in lovingkindness and mercy, and in faithfulness. Thank You for blessing me to know You as Your betrothed. May my heart belong to You, never to be separated from Your love. The poem, "Sunday Love," speaks of how I long to be in Your presence:

> "You only come on Sunday
>   But so it really does seem
> Monday through Saturday are nothing
>   But on Sunday You're a dream.
>
> If only I could have You, Lord,
>   Each and every day

I'd be everything to You
    I'd do anything You say.

I don't want any more days like this
    I'm lonely for Your touch
I want You ever near me
    I love You ever so much.

Hold me close and love me
    Each and every day
Won't You come more often
    And, Lord, please come to stay.

I know that You love me
    For You've shown me again and again
With all my heart, mind, and strength
    I'll love You the best I can."

Again, Father, thank You for having me as Your betrothed. To You, O Lord, be all glory, honor, and praise! In Jesus' holy and precious name I pray. Amen.

3

Poems Reflecting the Betrothed

(Taken from the book *Caught Up in His Love*, by Leslie Johnson, 1987)

The Groom

You need not worry or give a care
For there is no pain that I cannot bear.

I'll bear your burdens and my own
I'll indeed reap what you have sown.

You are my bride, my life, my love
You are to me a perfect dove.

I'll love and hold you very tight
I'll never let you out of sight.

For you I'll fight and for you I'll die
And it is indeed you who can make me cry.

I'm tougher than tough and weaker than weak
And it is indeed I whom all men seek.

Yet, you have found me and we've become as one
You and I and the Son.

Bride and Groom

You are my bride and I your groom
I'll come as lightning and make it soon.

Together we will forever be
Loving each other for all to see.

Tongues will wag but who's to care
No greater love for us to share.

We have loved for many years
Through laughter and through many tears.

Now the time has arrived
For our love through time has survived.

LESLIE J. DRUMMOND

And There Was Love

        Peace
        Tranquility
        Serenity
Her soul reached to His
        Enmeshed
        Intertwined
        Fused
They became one Soul
        Cosmically
        Universally
        One —Love.

I'm Yours Forever

Love me tender
    Love me long

Love me forever
    In a song.

I'll love you long
    I'll love you hard

No more for us to
    Ever part.

You are my bride
    Forever to be.

No greater love
    Anywhere for me.

I am yours
    And yours forever

Through stormy times
    Or indeed whatever.

Loving You

Loving you is so easy for me
Loving you makes me feel so free.
Free to walk, free to care,
Free to talk, free to share.
I love you deeply and this is true,
I'll love forever the Son in you.

LESLIE J. DRUMMOND

Will You Love Me Tomorrow?

When silver streaks my hair
    Will you love me tomorrow?

When my skin is no longer fair
    Will you love me tomorrow?

When my bones creak as I walk
    Will you love me tomorrow?

When old age slows me almost to a halt
    Will you love me tomorrow?

I ask again, "Will you love me tomorrow?"

Indeed, I'll Love You Forever

I'll love you when your hair falls out
    When your midriff spreads
        And your shoulders hunch.

I'll love you when your hearing weakens
    And when with disease
        You are stricken.

I'll love you despite what comes
    I'll not only love you
        When you are well
I'll even love you when you are ill.

Indeed, I'll love you
    Forever.

How I'll Love You

    I long to hold you
        In my arms
    And keep you safe
        From all harm.

    I'll keep you close
        In tender care
    I'll show you that my love
        Is fair.

    I want you to forever
        Be mine
    And to you, darling,
        I will be kind.

    I'll give to you
        All that I can

LESLIE J. DRUMMOND

Darling, I am your
>   Number one fan.

I'll show you a love
>   That can't be bought
I'll love you like
>   A man ought.

I'll give to you
>   The best of me
An unending love
>   Forever free.

Love me, darling,
>   And never let go
For my love to you
>   I'll ever show.

4

A Selection of Prayers Adapted to God's Word

Praying for Children and Parenting

Heavenly Father, God of all creation, Almighty and Eternal God! We thank You and praise You for Your goodness to all, and Your tender mercies upon all Your works. We thank You for our children. May they all be taught of You, O Lord, and find the great peace therein. May they hearken unto their fathers that begot them and despise not their mothers when their mothers are old. For we can have no greater joy than to hear that our children are walking in the truth.

Your Word tells us that You will pour water upon him that is thirsty, and floods upon dry ground: You will pour Your Spirit upon our seed, and Your blessing upon our offspring. And they shall spring up as among the grass, as willows by the water courses.

May we have no guilt or condemnation about the mistakes we have made as parents, for Your word tells us that "there is therefore now no condemnation to those who are in Christ Jesus, who do not walk according to the flesh, but according to the Spirit." Help us to walk daily in the Spirit.

Help us, O Lord, to train our children in the way they should go so that when they are old, they will not depart from it.

Thank You for Your covenant with us, Your people, that says, "My Spirit which is upon you, and My words which I have put in your mouth shall not depart from your mouth, nor from the mouths of your seed, nor from the mouths of your seed's seed, now and forever."

All glory, honor, and praise to You, O Lord!

In Jesus' name we pray.

Amen.

Praying God's Word for Deliverance

Almighty and Eternal God! God who saves and delivers us from our destructions! Our fathers trusted in You, and You delivered them. We thank you and praise You for sending Jesus Christ, who gave Himself for our sins that He might deliver us from this present evil age.

Lord, Your word says that You will help them and deliver them from the wicked because they trust in You. Do not make us a reproach of the foolish. Be pleased to deliver us; O Lord, make haste to help us. Help us to remember that in the time of trouble, You, Lord, will deliver those who consider the poor. Again, we pray: Make haste, O Lord, to deliver us! Make haste to help us! Your Word further tells us that You will deliver the needy when they cry, the poor also, and him who has no helper.

Help us to be mindful of Your Word that says, "Because he has set his love upon Me, therefore I will deliver him. I will set him on high because he has known My name. He shall call upon Me and I will answer him and honor him. With long life I will satisfy him and show him My salvation."

Thank You for delivering our souls from lying lips and deceitful tongues. Thank You for delivering us from our enemies and preserving us from violent men. Lord, we trust not in ourselves but in You who raises the dead, delivering us from death. So, we wait for Your Son from heaven, whom You raised from the dead, Jesus, who delivers us from the wrath to come.

Thank You, O God, for delivering us from every evil work and preserving us for Your heavenly kingdom. To You be all glory, honor, and praise!

In Jesus' holy and precious name.

Amen.

Praying God's Word on Faith

Almighty and Eternal God! Blessed is Your holy name! We thank You and praise You for every good gift that comes down from heaven, and that with You there is no shadow of turning. We thank You for the gift of faith to trust, believe, and depend on You; thank You for giving each of us a measure of faith.

Your Word tells us that faith is the substance of things hoped for, the evidence of things not seen. And without faith, it is impossible to please You. For he who comes to you must believe that You are. Teach us, O God, how to walk by faith in Your Word and not by sight, for Your Word is truth. Your Word says, "The just shall live by faith." Help us to live trusting and believing that what Your Word says, You will do. Let us not lean to our own understanding; but instead, let us lean and rely totally on You.

Give us a hunger and thirst for Your Word, for we understand that "faith comes by hearing and hearing by the Word of God." Moreover, help us to learn how to use our faith to quench the fiery darts of the wicked one; for as we resist him, he will flee.

May we come to understand that whatever is born of You, O God, overcomes the world. And this is the victory that overcomes the world— our faith.

To You, O Lord, we give all glory, honor, and praise!
In the holy name of Jesus.
Amen.

Praying God's Word on Faithfulness

O Lord, You are our God! We will exalt You; we will praise Your name for You have done wonderful things. Your counsels of old are faithfulness and truth. Your mercies are new every morning. Great is Your faithfulness!

Thank You, Lord, for betrothing us to Yourself in faithfulness so that we may know You. Help us to declare Your faithfulness and Your salvation, not concealing Your lovingkindness and truth from the great assembly. May we sing of Your mercies, making known Your faithfulness forever.

O Lord God of hosts, who is mighty like You? Your Word tells us that Your faithfulness surrounds You. May we always sing praises to Your name, declaring Your lovingkindness in the morning and Your faithfulness at night. Thank You that Your faithfulness endures to all generations.

Hear our prayer, O Lord. Thank You for giving ear to our supplications. For in Your faithfulness You will surely answer us. May we remember that if we confess our sins, You are faithful and just to forgive us our sins and to cleanse us from all unrighteousness. And You are faithful to sanctify us completely and preserve our whole spirit, soul, and body blameless at the coming of our Lord Jesus Christ. Thank You for establishing us and guarding us from the evil one.

Now, Lord, let us hold fast the confession of our hope without wavering; for You, O Lord, who promised, are faithful.

All glory, honor, and praise to You, Lord God!
In the holy and blessed name of Jesus we pray.
Amen.

Praying God's Word on Forgiveness

Heavenly Father! Lord God Most High! Creator and Sustainer of all things in heaven and on earth! We thank You and praise You for You are good to all, and Your tender mercies are over all Your works! Your Word tells us that You are good, ready to forgive, and abundant in mercy to all who call upon You. We thank You that by grace through faith in Christ Jesus, we have redemption through His blood: the forgiveness of sins. If You, Lord, should mark iniquities, who could stand? But with You there is forgiveness.

Help us, Lord, to be kind to one another, tenderhearted, forgiving one another, as You, God in Christ, forgave us. We are taught that if we forgive men their trespasses, You, our Heavenly Father will also forgive us. But if we do not forgive men their trespasses, neither will You forgive us our trespasses. Moreover, Your Word teaches us that when we stand praying and recall that we have something against another, we must forgive him, that You, Father may also forgive us.

When our brother sins against us and we rebuke him, and then he repents, remind us, prompt us, and help us to forgive him. And if he sins against us seven times in a a day and seven times in a day repents, lead us to forgive him. For if we confess our sins, You, O Lord, are faithful and just to forgive us our sins and to cleanse us from all unrighteousness. Thank You for forgiving us for Your name's sake and removing our transgressions from us as far as the east is from the west.

To You, O Lord, be all glory, honor, and praise!

In Jesus' holy name we pray.

Amen.

Praying God's Word on Grace

Almighty and Eternal God! Father and Creator of all! God of faithfulness, compassion, and grace! To You, O Lord, we give thanks and praise! Thank You for the gift of grace, Your unmerited favor and compassion by which we are saved from judgment through faith in Jesus Christ. Thank You that grace, ministered by the

Holy Spirit, brings power to not only save us, but also to enable us to live holy lives and to do Your will.

We thank You and praise You that when we are weak, Your grace is sufficient; for Your strength is made perfect in our weakness. May we always turn to You for strength, knowing that we can receive, by grace, Your Providential care.

Thank You for pouring grace upon our households, taking us from glory to glory. May we come to know through experience what it means to have great grace upon us, as the apostles of old knew. We thank You, Lord, for blessing us to receive abundance of grace and the gift of righteousness through Jesus Christ.

May we not be tempted to be made righteous by self-efforts, but instead remember that we are made righteous by the finished works of Jesus on the cross. Help us to grow in grace and knowledge of our Lord and Savior Jesus Christ. Your Word tells us that "You resist the proud, but give grace to the humble." May grace be with all who love our Lord Jesus Christ in sincerity.

To You, O Lord God, we give all glory, honor, and praise!

In the holy name of Jesus we pray.

Amen.

Praying God's Word for Health and Healing

Almighty and Eternal God! God Most High! Creator and Sustainer of all life! All glory, honor, and praise to You—The Lord who Heals!

Thank You for sending Your only begotten Son, Jesus Christ, who through Your gift of salvation brought healing and health to us. Your Word tells us that by His stripes we were healed. While we thank You for the men and women who practice medicine in an effort to heal our bodies, we realize that ultimately healing comes from You. Your Word tells us that "You sent Your Word and healed us and delivered us from our destructions."

Help us to focus on Your Word, for it has power to heal even a broken heart, as well as bind up wounds; to give life and health to the flesh; and make us whole. As we anticipate the manifestation of healing, may we be mindful to turn to You, the Great Physician who created us in our mother's womb. Give us a sincere desire to seek You in Your Word and to magnify Your Word above our sicknesses and diseases, for You magnify Your Word even above Your name.

We believe that all power is in Your hand, and with You nothing shall be impossible. Moreover, Your arm is not shortened that You cannot reach into our situation, nor is Your ear too dull to hear us when we pray.

Thank You for being no respecter of persons, which tells us that healing is available to us, as well as to others. We know by Your Word that You are the same yesterday, today, and forever and that You care for us.

Now, Lord, may we prosper and be in health even as our souls prosper.

Again, to You, O Lord, be all glory, honor, and praise! In Jesus' holy name we pray.

Amen.

Praying God's Word on Hope

Almighty and Eternal God! Our Creator and Sustainer! God of our hope! Blessed be the God and Father of our Lord Jesus Christ, who according to His abundant mercy has begotten us again to a living hope through the resurrection of Jesus Christ from the dead, to an inheritance incorruptible and undefiled and that does not fade away, reserved in heaven for us who are kept by the power of God through faith for salvation, ready to be revealed in the last time.

Your Word tells us that it is good to have hope and wait quietly for the salvation of the Lord. You are our portion; therefore, we have hope in You. Our hearts are glad, and our glory rejoices. Our flesh will rest in hope. Moreover, we are reminded by the Psalmist to be of good courage, for You will strengthen our hearts, all who hope in You. And further, it is said that Your eye is on those who fear You and hope in Your mercy. Let Your mercy be upon, just as we hope in You.

Thank You that the hope of the righteous will be gladness. We will, therefore, hope continually and praise You yet more and more. May we always set our hope in you and not forget Your works, as the Holy Spirit leads us in keeping Your commandments.

We wait for You, O Lord God, our souls wait, and in Your Word we do hope. You are our trust from our youth. Now may You, the God of hope, fill us with all joy and peace in believing that we may abound in hope by the power of the Holy Spirit. And we thank You for Christ in us, the hope of glory.

To You, Lord, be all glory, praise, and honor.

In Jesus' holy name.

Amen.

Praying God's Word for Justice

Heavenly Father! Eternal God Most High! Holy is Your name! Lord, we thank You and praise You for Your goodness to all and Your tender mercies over all Your works. We thank You and praise You that Your hand is not shortened that it cannot save, nor Your ear heavy that it cannot hear. Thank You for being a God of justice and righteousness.

Thank You for bringing forth Your righteousness as the light and Your justice as the noonday. Thank You for bringing justice to the poor, saving the children of the needy, and breaking the oppressors. We thank You for making justice the measuring line.

Help us, Lord, to keep justice and do righteousness, following after Your Elect One (Jesus Christ) in whom Your soul delights! Your Word tells us that You have put Your Spirit upon Him and He will bring justice to the Gentiles. He will bring forth justice for truth. He will not fail nor be discouraged, till He has established justice in the earth.

May we execute true justice, show compassion and mercy, everyone to his brother. Let us not oppress the widow or the fatherless, the alien or the poor. And let none of us plan evil in our heart against our brother, remembering that the foundation of Your throne is justice and righteousness. Also, that to do righteousness and justice is more acceptable to You than sacrifice.

All glory, honor and praise to You, O God!
In Jesus' holy name.
Amen.

Praying God's Word on Love

Almighty and Eternal God! Our Creator and Redeemer! God of mercy and compassion! God of love!

Blessed is Your holy name! We worship You for who You are, the only true and living God!

Thank You for so loving the whole world that You gave Your only begotten Son so that we who believe on Him should not perish but have eternal life, which is knowing You and the One You have sent.

Help us to obey Jesus' new commandment "to love one another as He has loved us." Thank You, Father, for sending the Holy Spirit to shed Your love abroad in our hearts. May we submit to the Holy Spirit as He leads and guides us in the way of love, remembering that love suffers long and is kind; love does not envy, nor parade itself, nor is it puffed up. It does not behave rudely, does not seek its own, and is not easily provoked. Moreover, love thinks no evil, does no evil; love bears all things, believes all things, hopes all things, endures all things. Love never fails.

May we, like Christ Jesus, show no partiality, but love even our enemies. Increase our understanding regarding the saying: "Greater love has no one than this, than to lay down one's life for his friends" so that we can walk in this love.

And may we never leave You, our First Love.

To You, O Lord, be all glory, honor, and praise!

In Jesus' holy name.

Amen.

A Woman's Prayer for Marriage in Christ Jesus

Heavenly Father, our Creator and Sustainer! Almighty and Eternal God! Holy is Your name!

I thank You and praise You for Your goodness and mercy that follow me all the days of my life and that Your mercies are new every morning. Great is Your faithfulness! And for Your goodness over all Your works, I give You thanks and praise!

Among the many blessings You have made available to mankind is the holy union of a man and a woman. For Your Word tells us that it is not good for man to be alone, so You created woman, a comparable helper to him. Moreover, Your Word says, "Therefore, a man shall leave his father and mother and be joined to his wife, and they shall become one flesh." Lord, help me to become a suitable wife for a godly man, who loves You and is filled with the Holy Spirit, who keeps You first in his life, and who vows to love, honor, and cherish a wife, as Christ also loved the church and gave Himself for her.

May I love, honor, and respect him, showering him with the sweet, gentle, tenderness of Christ Jesus. May we both put the interests and concerns of each other before our own. And may we pray daily for one another.

Thank You, Lord, for the Holy Spirit, our Helper and Sustainer. Without hesitation, may we both listen and follow His wisdom and guidance, knowing that His words are aligned with Your written Word. When we find it difficult to submit to the other, let us recall that we can do all things through Christ who strengthens us, and that we are called to submit to one another in the fear and reverence of God, not demanding our own way, but following God's way. Enable my husband and me to put on tender mercies, kindness, humility, meekness, long-suffering, forgiveness, faithfulness, and love which is the bond of perfection. And let the peace of God rule in our hearts.

May I become a virtuous wife, as described in Proverbs 31.

May my worth be far above rubies, and my husband be able to safely trust in me, having no lack of gain. May I do him good and never evil all the days of my life, working diligently to make a pleasant and comfortable home. And may I always extend my hand to the needy. Establish my husband as a well-respected member of the community. May he be known for his kindness, wisdom, integrity, and generosity.

Now Lord, may my love and service to others bring glory, honor, and praise to You!

All these things I ask in the holy and precious name of Jesus Christ.

Amen.

Praying God's Word on Mercy

Lord God of heaven, O great and awesome God! You who keep covenant and mercy with those who love You and observe Your commandments, be attentive and open Your eyes so that You may hear our prayer. In Your mercy, help us to reverence Your name. Help us to humble ourselves, pray and seek Your face, and turn from our wicked ways. For then You will hear from heaven, forgive our sins, and heal our land. Have mercy on us and hear our prayer, for You, O God, are rich in mercy.

Help us to follow Your paths, for all Your paths are mercy and truth to those who keep Your covenant and testimonies. Your Word tells us that many sorrows shall be to the wicked, but he who trusts in You, O Lord, mercy surrounds him. Thank You that Your eye is on those who fear You and have hope in Your mercy. Let Your mercy be upon us as we hope in You. Show us Your mercy, Lord, and grant us Your salvation. For You are good and ready to forgive, and abundant in mercy to all those who call upon You. Thank You that when our foot slips, Your mercy will hold us up.

Merciful God, we thank You that "as the heavens are high above the earth, so great is Your mercy toward those who fear You." We praise You and thank You that You are good to all and Your tender mercies are over all Your works. May we, too, show mercy toward others, especially the poor, recalling that he who follows righteousness and mercy finds life, righteousness, and honor.

Thank You, Lord, for showing us what You require of us: To do justly, to love mercy, and to walk humbly with our God. May we show mercy with cheerfulness. Thank You for saving us according to Your mercy, through the washing of regeneration and renewing of the Holy Spirit whom You poured on us abundantly through Jesus Christ our Savior, that having been justified by His grace we should become heirs according to the hope of eternal life.

Glory to You, O Lord!
In Jesus' name.
Amen.

A Prayer for Our Pastors

Almighty and Eternal God, Creator of heaven and earth and all things therein! Holy is Your name! We praise You and give You thanks to You for Your mercy endures forever; Your love never fails nor ends. Great is Your faithfulness!

Thank You for sending us a shepherd, [_____],
to [_____Church]

to lead, guide, teach, exhort, and love us, Your people. May he walk before You in truth, in righteousness, and in uprightness of heart. May he be faithful over the few until You make him servant over many.

Give our pastor an understanding heart full of knowledge and wisdom so that he may shepherd Your flock according to Your will. Watch over him day and night; keep his heart and mind stayed on You, for then You will give him perfect peace.

May Your Word be his meditation day and night. Restrain his feet from every evil way, that he may keep Your Word. May Your Word always be sweet to his taste and more desirable than anything on earth. For You exalt Your Word even above Your name.

May our pastor always abide under the shadow of Your wing, taking refuge in You. Thank You for giving Your angels charge over him to keep him in all his ways. May he prosper in all things and be in health, even as his soul prospers. And may he know the love of Christ which passes knowledge and be filled with all the fullness of You, O Lord God.

Thank You for the calling on his life and the genuine faith that is in him, which dwelt in his forefathers and mothers. May he, without fail, be loyal to the faith, being obedient to the leading of the Holy Spirit who dwells in him.

Help him to keep himself cleansed from youthful lusts, but pursue righteousness, faith, love, and peace.

Enable him, by Your Spirit, to avoid foolish and ignorant disputes, knowing that they generate strife. Grant him the grace to be gentle to all, patient, and able to walk in virtuous behavior before all mankind. May humility be one of his distinguishing characteristics as a disciple of Christ Jesus.

Further, Father, may our shepherd on earth always be sober-minded, hospitable, not given to wine, not violent, nor greedy for money, nor quarrelsome. Help him to order every area of his life: 1) how to balance his ministry, 2) how to manage on-the-job stress, 3) how to keep the home fires burning, and 4) how to safeguard his sexual integrity.

May he always be strong in the grace that is in Christ Jesus.

To You, O Lord, be all glory, honor, and praise!

These and all blessings we ask in Jesus' name.

Amen.

Praying God's Word on Patience

Heavenly Father, God of patience and comfort! Grant us to be like-minded, showing patience toward one another in all things. Thank You for giving Jesus Christ to us as an example of long-suffering when He patiently endured the Cross. Praise be to You, O Lord!

Help us by patience to possess our souls, remaining calm and composed in trials. Help us to hear Your Word with a noble and good heart, keeping it and bearing fruit with patience. And not only this, but with joy let us exult in our sufferings and rejoice in our hardships, knowing that hardship (distress, pressure, and trouble) produces patient endurance. As we hope for what we do not see, help us to wait for it eagerly with patience and composure, remembering that through the patience and composure of the Scriptures, we have hope.

Lord, according to Christ's glorious power, strengthen us with all might to be patient and long-suffering with joy. May we learn to count it all joy when we fall into various trials, knowing that the testing of our faith produces patience. May we let patience have its perfect work, that we may be perfect and complete, lacking nothing.

Enable us to be patient until the coming of the Lord. Let us not grumble against one another lest we be condemned. May we remember the prophets who spoke in the name of the Lord as examples of suffering and patience.

Help us to remember Your Word that a man's wisdom gives him patience; it is to his glory to overlook an offense.

Thank You, Lord, for the wisdom that gives patience.

All glory, honor, and praise to You, O Lord, today and forever!

In Jesus' holy name.

Amen.

Praying God's Word on Peace

Heavenly Father, Creator God! Almighty One of righteousness, joy, and peace! Holy is Your name. Blessed and Exalted God Most High! We praise You and thank You for making Your peace within our reach in this world.

Your Word tells us that You will keep him in perfect peace whose mind is stayed on You, because he trusts in You. Moreover, Jesus gave us His peace, so that our hearts need not be troubled. Help us to know this peace—the peace of Christ that will guard our hearts and minds, surpassing all understanding.

May we recall that when a man's ways please You, O Lord, You make even his enemies to be at peace with him. Help us to pursue peace with all people. Further, may we daily depart from evil and do good, consciously and decidedly seeking peace for our lives, realizing that the meek shall inherit the earth and delight themselves in the abundance of peace. Help us to remember that the blameless, upright man has a future of peace.

Thank You, Lord, for the great peace that comes to us who love Your law, obeying Your Word. May we spend time daily abiding therein, for there we will find wisdom that leads to paths of peace.

Now, Lord, may You bless us; make Your face shine upon us and be gracious to us. Thank You for lifting Your countenance upon us and giving us peace.

All glory, honor, and praise to You, O Lord!

In Jesus' holy name we pray.

Amen.

Praying God's Word on Provision

Almighty and Eternal God! Our Creator and Sustainer! God Most High! God our Provider! Holy is Your name!

Lord, we thank You and praise You that You visit the earth and water it; Your river is full of water. And You provide our grain, for so You have prepared it. You even provide water from rocks so that the waters gush out and overflow streams. And when we cannot see how to provide for ourselves, You always "see provision" and provide for us. As it is said to this day, "In the Mount of the Lord, it shall be provided."

May we do as Jesus instructed His disciples, saying, "Do not worry about your life, what you will eat, nor about your body, what you will put on. Life is more than food, and the body is more than clothing." "Do not fear, for it is your Father's good pleasure to give you the kingdom." "Seek first the kingdom of God and His righteousness, and all these things will be added to you.

Therefore, do not worry about tomorrow, for tomorrow will worry about its own things. Sufficient for the day is its own trouble."

Further, Lord, thank You for being our Shepherd so that we shall not want or be without. Thank You for providing a place of calmness and serenity to restore our souls. Thank You for providing and leading us in paths of righteousness. Thank You for providing us a sense of security by Your comforting presence. And thank You for providing us with Your goodness and mercy that follow us all the days of our lives.

Your Word tells us that no good thing will You withhold from those who walk uprightly. Therefore, let us put our trust in You and Your word that promises—"My Lord shall provide all my need according to His riches in glory by Christ Jesus."

To You, O Lord, be all glory, honor, and praise forever!
In Jesus' holy name.
Amen.

Praying God's Word for Strength

Father in heaven, Most High God! God of gods! Lord of lords! King of kings! The only true God! We give You thanks and praise for never leaving us nor forsaking us. Therefore, we need never fear, for You are our God.

Thank You for strengthening us and assuring us of Your help. Thank You for taking hold of us with Your righteous right hand—a hand of justice, power, victory, and salvation.

May we forever recall that though our flesh and our heart fail, You, O Lord, are the strength of our heart and our portion for all times, and that the joy of the Lord is our strength.

Thank You for giving strength to Your people and blessing Your people with peace. Help us not to forget that we can do all things through Christ who strengthens us, and that You sent the Holy Spirit to live in us as Helper, Sustainer, Intercessor, Advocate, Comforter, and Strengthener.

To You, God Almighty, be all glory, honor, and praise! In Jesus' name.

Amen.

Praying God's Word on Thanksgiving

Heavenly Father, Creator God and Sustainer of all things in heaven and on earth! Omnipotent, Omniscient, Omnipresent God! To You we give thanks and praise! Blessed be Your holy name! For Your mercy endures forever and Your love never ends.

We come into Your presence with thanksgiving, making a joyful noise to You with words of praise. We bless Your holy name. For You sent Your Word and healed us, and delivered us from our destructions. May we offer thanksgiving sacrifices and tell of Your deeds with joy. We thank You for executing justice for the oppressed and giving food to the hungry. But most of all, O God, we thank You for giving us Your only begotten Son that whosoever believes on Him shall not perish, but have everlasting life. Thank You that He came not to judge the world, but to save the world. Moreover, we thank You that He came that we might have life and have it more abundantly.

Further, we thank You for the Holy Spirit, the Spirit of truth, our Helper, who abides in us forever. Thank You that He serves as Comforter, Advocate, Intercessor, Counselor, Strengthener, and Stand-by. Thank You that He guides us into all truth.

Now, Lord, for the love of Christ that passes knowledge and the peace that surpasses all understanding, we give You praise and thanksgiving today and forever.

To You be all glory, honor, and praise!

In Jesus' name.

Amen.

Praying God's Word on Truth

Heavenly Father, Maker of heaven and earth! Omnipotent, Omniscient, Omnipresent God! The only true God! We exalt You and praise Your holy name!

We come to You with thanksgiving and praise for sending truth to mankind. Your Word tells us that You are spirit and he who worships You must do so in spirit and truth. Thank You for sending truth to us by Jesus Christ —the word made flesh, full of grace and truth. According to Your Word, Jesus said, "If you abide in My Word, you are My disciples indeed. And you shall know the truth, and the truth shall set you free."

Lord, give us a desire for Your Word. May reading, studying, meditating, and praying Your Word of truth become an important part of our daily lives. Help us to develop a love for truth, for we are sanctified by Your truth, as well as shielded and protected by it. May we understand clearly and accept that Jesus is the way, the truth, and the life. And that no one gets to You except by Him.

Further, Lord, we thank You for the Holy Spirit, the Spirit of truth, our Helper and Comforter who will guide us into all truth, and on Christ's authority will even tell us of things to come.

Again, O Lord, thank You for blessing us with truth.
All glory, honor, and praise to You, O Most High God!
In Jesus' holy and precious name we pray.
Amen.

Praying God's Word for Unity

Heavenly Father, Most High God! Creator of heaven and earth!

We praise You and thank You for the divine oneness of all things. We are reminded of Jesus' prayer for all believers, "that we would all be one, as He and You, Father—You in Him, and Him in You." Lord, may we be one in You and in the Son, as Jesus prayed that we would be made perfect in one.

The Psalmist reminds us of "how good and how pleasant it is for brethren to dwell together in unity!" He describes it as "precious oil upon the head, running down the beard; and like dew descending upon the mountains of Zion; for there You, O Lord, commanded the blessing—Life forevermore."

May we come to appreciate and treasure unity among the brethren, endeavoring to keep the unity of the Spirit in the bond of peace. To this end, may we learn to walk worthy of the call with which we were called, with lowliness and gentleness, with long-suffering, bearing with one another in love, and remembering that there is one God and Father of all, who is above all, and in us all.

To You, O Lord, we give You all glory, honor, and praise!

In Jesus' holy name we pray.

Amen.

Prayer of Praise and Thanksgiving for God's Word

Almighty and Eternal God, Creator and Sustainer of heaven and earth! We praise You and thank You for Your Word, for the Bible tells us that Your Word is truth and that it is very near to us, in our mouth, and in our heart, that we may do it.

Your Word also tells us that man shall not live by bread alone, but live by every word that proceeds from Your mouth, O God. May we learn to trust You at Your word, for it reminds us that "You are not man that You should lie, nor a son of man that You should repent. Have You not said, and will You to make it good?"

We thank You and praise You that "when Your Word goes forth from Your mouth, it shall not return to You void. But it shall accomplish what You please and it shall prosper in the thing for which You sent it." Thank You for performing Your purpose, fulfilling Your word.

Heighten our trust in You, for Your Word is pure, a shield to those who put their trust in You. We praise You, for Your way is perfect; Your Word is proven; and is a shield to all who trust in You. We praise You that by Your Word, the heavens were made, and all the host of them by the breath of Your mouth.

Whenever fear comes, we will put our trust in You. We will praise Your Word. In You will we trust and not fear for we know that You love the whole world. Thank You, Lord, for the angels who excel in strength, who do Your Word, heeding the voice of Your Word. You sent Your Word and healed us and delivered us from our destructions.

Your Word is a comfort in our afflictions, for it has given us life. Thank You for being merciful to us according to Your Word. Before we were afflicted, we went astray. But now we keep Your Word.

Heavenly Father, we rejoice at Your Word as one who finds a great treasure. May we meditate in Your Word day and night. And may we also speak Your Word, for You have magnified Your Word above all Your name. 30

We are reminded that Jesus cast out spirits with a word and healed all who were sick. The Bible tells us that "the Word of God is living and powerful." And that forever Your Word is settled in heaven.

To You, O Lord God, be all glory, honor, and praise forever!

In Jesus' holy and precious name, we pray.

Amen.

Scripture References by Prayer

(Unless otherwise indicated, Scriptures were taken from the New King James Version of the Bible, copyright 1982 by Thomas Nelson, Inc. Used by permission. All rights reserved.)

1. Prayer for Children and Parenting—Psalm 145:13; Isaiah 54:13; Proverbs 23:22; III John 1:4; Isaiah 44:3-4; Romans 8:1; Proverbs 22:6; and Isaiah 59:21.
2. Prayer for Deliverance—Psalm 107:20; Psalm 22:4; Galatians 1:4; Psalm 37:40; Psalm 39:8; Psalm 40:13; Psalm 41:1; Psalm 70:1; Psalm 91:14-15; Psalm 120:2; II Corinthians 1:9-10; I Thessalonians 1:10; and II Timothy 4:18.
3. Prayer on Faith— James 1:17; Romans 12:3; Hebrews 11:1; Hebrews 11:6; II Corinthians 5:7; John 17:17; Ga-

latians 3:11 and Hebrews 10:38; Numbers 23:19; Proverbs 3:5a; Romans 10:17; Ephesians 6:16; James 4:7; I John 5:4.

4. Prayer on Faithfulness— Isaiah 25:1; Lamentations 3:23; Hosea 2:20; Psalm 40:10; Psalm 89:1; Psalm 89:8; Psalm 92:2; Psalm 119:90a; Psalm 143:1; I John 1:9; I Thessalonians 5:23; II Thessalonians 3:3; and Hebrews 10:23.

5. Prayer on Forgiveness—Psalm 145:9; Psalm 86:5; Ephesians 2:8; Psalm 130:3-4a; Ephesians 4;32; Matthew 6:14-15; Mark 11:25; Luke 17:3; I John 1:9; I John 2:12; and Psalm 103:12.

6. Prayer on Grace— Ephesians 2:8; Ephesians 2:10; II Corinthians 12:9; Psalm 84:11; Acts 4:33; Romans 5:17; Galatians 5:4; II Peter 3:18; James 4:6; and Ephesians 6:24.

7. Prayer for Health and Healing— Exodus 15:26; I Peter 2:24; Isaiah 53:5; Psalm 107:20; Psalm 147:3; Proverbs 4:22; Luke 17:19; Psalm 139:13; Psalm 138:2; Luke 1:37; Isaiah 59:1; Acts 10:34; Hebrews 13:8; and III John 2.

8. Prayer for Hope— Romans 15:13; I Peter 1:3-5; Lamentations 3:26; Lamentations 3:24; Psalm 16:9; Psalm 31:24; Psalm 33:18; Psalm 33:22; Proverbs 10:28a; Psalm 71:14; Psalm 78;7; Psalm 130:5; Psalm 42:5b; Psalm 71:5; Romans 15:13; and Colossians 1:27. 32

9. Prayer for Justice— Psalm 145:9; Isaiah 59:1; Isaiah 30:18; Psalm 37:6; Psalm 72:4; Isaiah 28:17a; Isaiah 56:1; Matthew 12:18b; Isaiah 42:1c; Isaiah 42:3-4; Zechariah 7:9-10; Psalm 89:14; and Proverbs 21:3.
10. Prayer on Love—I John 4:8; John 3:16; John 17:3; John 13:34; John 15:12; Romans 5:5; I Corinthians 13:4-8; Acts 10:34; Luke 6:37; John 15:13; Proverbs 10:12b; Psalm 91: 14-16 and Revelation 2:4.
11. Prayer for Marriage in Christ Jesus (NKJV)—Psalm 23:6; Lamentations 3:23; Psalm 145: 9; Genesis 2:18; Genesis 2:24; Ephesians 5:25; Ephesians 5:33; I Corinthians 13:5; Colossians 4:2b; John 15:26; John 16: 12-15; Philippians 4:13; Ephesians 5:21; I Corinthians 13:5; Colossians 3:12-15 and Proverbs 31:10-31.
12. Prayer for Mercy—Nehemiah 1:5-6; II Chronicles 7:14; Psalm 4:1; Ephesians 2:4; Psalm 25:10; Psalm 32:10; Psalm 33:18, 22; Psalm 85:7; Psalm 86:5; Psalm 94:18; Psalm 103:11; Psalm 145:9; Proverbs 21:21; Micah 6:8; Romans 12:8 and Titus 3:5.
13. Praying for Our Pastors—Psalm 106:1; Psalm 107:2; I Corinthians 13:8; Lamentations 3:23; I Kings 3:6; Matthew 25:23; I Kings 3:9; Isaiah 26:3; Psalm 119:101; Psalm 119:103; Psalm 138:2; Psalm 91:4; Psalm 91:11; III John 2; Ephesians 3:19; II Timothy 1:5; II Timothy 1:14; II Timothy 2::21-25; I Timothy 3:2-3 and II Timothy 2:1.

14. Prayer for Peace—Isaiah 26:3; John 14:27; Philippians 4:7; Proverbs 16:7; Hebrews 12:14; Psalm 34:14; Psalm 37:11; Psalm 37:37; Psalm 119:165; Proverbs 16:7 and Numbers 6:24-26.
15. Prayer for Provision—Psalm 65:9; Psalm 78:20; Genesis 22:8; Genesis 22:14; Luke 12:22-23; Luke 12: 32; Matthew 6:33-34; Psalm 23:1; Psalm 23:2-6; Psalm 84:11b and Philippians 4:19.
16. Prayer for Patience—Romans 5:5; Romans 15:5; Luke 21:19; Luke 8:15; Romans 5:3; Romans 8:25 (AMP); Romans 15:4; Colossians 1:11; James 1:2; James 1:4; James 5:7; James 5:9-10 and Proverbs 19:11.
17. Prayer for Protection—Psalm 91:2; Lamentations 3:24; Psalm 145:9; Psalm 91:14-16; Psalm 91:1, 5-7; Proverbs 30:5; Psalm 119:114a; Psalm 84:11; Psalm 33:20; and Psalm 28:8-9b. 33
18. Prayer for Strength—Hebrews 13:5; Isaiah 41:10; Acts 18:10; Psalm 73:26; Nehemiah 8:10; Philippians 4:13 and John 15:26.
19. Prayer for Thanksgiving— Psalm 106;1; I Corinthians 13:8; Psalm 95:2; Psalm 107:20, 22; Psalm 146:7; John 3:16; John 12:47; John 10:10b; John 15:26 (AMP); Ephesians 3:19 and Philippians 4:7.
20. Prayer on Truth—John 1:14; John 4:24; John 1:14,17; John 8:31-32; John 17:17; Psalm 91:4b; John 14:6 and John 15:26.

21. Prayer for Unity—John 17:20-22; Psalm 133; Ephesians 4:3; and Ephesians 4:6.
22. Prayer of Praise and Thanksgiving for God's Word—John17:17; Deuteronomy 30:14; Deuteronomy 8:3; Matthew 4:4; Numbers 23:19; Isaiah 55:11; Lamentations 2:17; Psalm 119:105; Psalm 18:30; Psalm 33:6; Psalm 103:20; Psalm 107:20; Psalm 119:50, 58,67 162,148,172; Psalm 138:2; Matthew 8:16; Hebrews 4:12 and Psalm 119:89.

6

What the Bible Says about God's Word

The following Scriptures speak of God's Word:

1. In the beginning was the Word, and the Word was with God, and the Word was God (John 1:1).
2. By the Word of the Lord the heavens were made; and all the host of them by the breath of His mouth (Psalm 33:6).
3. Man shall not live by bread alone; but man lives by every word that proceeds from the mouth of the Lord (Deuteronomy 8:3; Matthew 4:4; Luke 4:4).
4. God is not man, that He should lie; nor a son of man, that He should repent. Has He not said, and will He not do? Or has He spoken, and will He not make it good? (Numbers 23:19).

5. Since you have purified your souls to obeying the truth through the Spirit in sincere love of the brethren, love one another fervently with a pure heart, having been born again, not of corruptible seed but incorruptible, through the Word of God which lives and abides forever (I Peter 1:22-23).
6. But the word is very near you, in your mouth and in your heart, that you may do it (Deuteronomy 30:14).
7. For as the rain comes down, and the snow from heaven, and do not return there, but water the earth, and make it bring forth bud, that it may give seed to the sower and bread to the eater, so shall My word be that goes forth from My mouth. It shall not return to Me void, but it shall accomplish what I please, and it shall prosper in the thing for which I sent it (Isaiah 55:10-11).
8. Then the Lord said to me, "You have seen well, for I am ready to perform My word." (Jeremiah 1:12).
9. The Lord has done what He purposed; He has fulfilled His word (Lamentations 2:17). 35
10. As for God, His way is perfect; the word of the Lord is proven; He is a shield to all who trust in Him (Psalm 18:30).
11. In God I will praise His word; in God I have put my trust; I will not fear: What can flesh do to me? (Psalm 56:4).

12. Bless the Lord, you His angels, who excel in strength, who do His word, heeding the voice of His word (Psalm 103:20).
13. He sent His word and healed them, and delivered them from their destructions (Psalm 107:20).
14. Remember the word to Your servant, upon which You have caused me to hope. This is my comfort in my affliction, for Your word has given me life (Psalm 119:49-50).
15. Before I was afflicted I went astray, but now I keep Your word (Psalm 119:67).
16. Your word is a lamp to my feet and a light to my path (Psalm 119:105).
17. Direct my steps by Your word, and let no iniquity have dominion over me (Psalm 119:133).
18. I wait for the Lord, my soul waits, and in His word I do hope (Psalm 130:5).
19. I will worship toward Your holy temple, and praise Your name for Your lovingkindness and Your truth; for You have magnified Your word above all Your name (Psalm 138:2).
20. My son, give attention to My words; incline your ear to my sayings. Do to let them depart from your eyes; keep them in the midst of your heart; for they are life to those who find them, and health to all their flesh (Proverbs 4:20-22).

21. And the Word became flesh and dwelt among us, and we beheld His glory, the glory as of the only begotten of the Father, full of grace and truth (John 1:14).
22. Sanctify them by Your truth. Your Word is truth (John 17:17).
23. Therefore lay aside all filthiness and overflow of wickedness, and receive with meekness the implanted word, which is able to save your souls (James 1:21).
24. So then faith comes by hearing, and hearing by the word of God (Romans 10:17).
25. And take the sword of the Spirit, which is the Word of God (Ephesians 6:17b).
26. For the Word of God is living and powerful and sharper than any two-edged sword, piercing even to the division of soul and spirit, and of joints and marrow, and is a discerner of the thoughts and intents of the heart (Hebrews 4:12).
27. The word is near you, in your mouth and in your heart, that is, the word of faith which we preach; that if you confess with your mouth the Lord Jesus and believe in your heart that God has raised Him from the dead, you will be saved (Romans 10:8-9).
28. But whoever keeps His Word, truly the love of God is perfected in him. By this we know that we are in Him (I John 2:5).

29. And they overcame him (the accuser of the brethren) by the blood of the Lamb and by the word of their testimony, and they did not love their lives to the death (Revelation 12:11).
30. He was clothed with a robe dipped in blood, and His name is called The Word of God (Revelation 19:13).

7

A Brief Commentary on Prayer

Why pray?

People pray for different reasons: for deliverance from pain and suffering; for peace of mind; for food, clothing, and shelter; for their marriage; for their children; for a job; for health and healing; and for myriad of other concerns and problems. Through the years, I have prayed these same issues of life and others that are not listed. But to state it plainly, I pray because I need God every day and in every area of my life.

I need God's wisdom to make wise and prudent decisions; His righteousness to be and do right; His unconditional love, mercy, compassion, peace, and forgiveness in order to love others as He loves me. More specifically, I pray 1) to communicate with God; 2) to express my adoration for Him; 3) to praise and thank Him;

4) to cast my cares on Him; 5) to hear a word from Him; 6) to make my requests known to Him; 7) to grow closer to God; 8) to spend quiet, quality time with God; 9) to learn about Him through personal experiences; and 10) to love on Him, one-on-One. Moreover, Jesus prayed, and I seek to follow the example of Christ Jesus.

Why Should I Pray God's Word?

Listed below are some plain and valid reasons why you should adapt your prayers to God's word:

1. First, in Isaiah 43:26, we are counseled to speak God's Word back to Him: "Let us contend together; state your case..."
2. God is His Word. Therefore, when you speak His Word in prayer, you are speaking to Him (see John 1:1).
3. Words have creative power. God spoke words when He created the heavens and earth (see Genesis 1:3).
4. The Word of God is truth (see John 17:17).
5. God will do what His Word says He will do (see Numbers 23:19).
6. God magnifies His Word above His name (see Psalm 138:2).

7. God's Word brings health to your flesh (see Proverbs 4:22).
8. God's words are life (see John 6:63).
9. You can pray with confidence that God hears you when you pray His Word (see I John 5:14-15).
10. God's Word heals and delivers us from destructions (see Psalm 107:20).
11. God's angels administer His Word (see Psalm 103:20).
12. God's Word is settled in heaven (see Psalm 119:89).
13. God's Word lights our way in this world (see Psalm 119:105).

As you become better acquainted with God's Word, you will discover a number of other reasons why you should pray His Word. Start today talking with God, thanking Him for His goodness and mercy to you and your loved ones. The more time you spend in God's Word, the more you will come to delight in Him.

How Should I Pray?

Pray from your heart. Praying is a personal act between you and God. And every one of us has our own personal issues and concerns. Moreover, the way you talk is not the way I talk. So be yourself and go to God, believing that He exists and trusting that He does what

He says He will do. If your believing is weak, ask God to help you to believe. And when you pray, do so with a reverent, respectful attitude. Be truthful with God; He is truthful with you in His Word.

In the beginning stages of your prayer life, you may find yourself praying just one word, such as, calling out the name of Jesus—"Jesus!" Or saying "Oh, God!" or "Lord, I need You!"

As a baby learns to talk to his mother, so we learn to talk, pray, and communicate with our Heavenly Father. When no one else knows what the baby is trying to communicate, the mother knows. Even more so, our Heavenly Father understands our attempts to pray, because He knows our hearts. So do not say, "I don't know how to pray." Start talking to your Heavenly Father. He will know the intentions of your heart, as well as what you are trying to say to Him. Trust God who is love, who created the universe, for He is All-knowing (Omniscient), All-powerful (Omnipotent), and Everywhere-present (Omnipresent) to hear our prayers.

Listed below are some commonly accepted suggestions to help you get started or grow in your prayer life:

1. Address our Heavenly Father with a reverent attitude.
2. Thank Him and praise Him for His goodness and mercy to you.

3. Ask Him to lead you to do His will for your life.
4. Say what you need (big or small).
5. Ask for forgiveness.
6. Consider asking a friend to sometimes pray with you.
7. Pray God's Word, adapting and including His Word in your prayer.
8. Take time to become familiar with Scripture.
9. Seek God's presence through "alone time" with Him.
10. Give God the glory and honor, and pray in the name of Jesus (not your own name).

When Should I Pray?

The Bible tells us to pray without ceasing. This could mean to pray/talk to God off and on as you go through your day—while working, walking, traveling, especially when you rise in the morning before you start your day, and before you fall asleep at night. Remember to pray before you eat a meal, thanking Him for and asking Him to bless your food. Make God your heavenly Partner in life. Stay in touch with Him at all times.

Where Should I Pray?

You may have heard that you should have a "prayer closet." While a private place where you can be alone with God is important, you can always create a sacred space in your mind to be with God wherever you find yourself. Become comfortable talking with God at all times and in all places. You do not have to wait until you arrive home after work, or even until bedtime. God is available to hear you at all times.

What Should I Pray About?

Pray about whatever is on your mind. Pray about your large, seemingly insurmountable problems, as well as things or matters you think are too small or insignificant to trouble God about. And pray for all things in between. Remember also to pray for others, including your enemies.

Some Benefits of Prayer

In summary, here are a few widely accepted benefits of prayer: Prayer—
1. Helps you develop a relationship with God.
2. Helps you gain an understanding of God's loving nature.
3. Provides answers and insight into many of life's problems.
4. Helps you find direction in your life.
5. Gives you strength to avoid temptation.

6. Aligns your will with God's will.
7. Can work miracles.
8. Can help you grow closer to God, accepting His will.
9. Invites the Holy Spirit into your life.
10. Helps you become more like Jesus.

A Sample Prayer for God's Presence

Heavenly Father, Creator God! Thank You for drawing us with Your love, reconciling us to friendship with You through Your only begotten Son, Jesus Christ. Thank You for welcoming us into Your presence where there is "fullness of joy and pleasures at Your right hand for ever more." Thank You that we can draw near to You with confidence, realizing that "he who dwells in the secret place of the Most High shall abide under the shadow of the Almighty, a place of refuge and protection." We praise You, for You are Omnipotent, Omniscient, and Omnipresent, even in the park. Thank you for the poem, "Love in the Park" which helps me to reflect being near You:

"Love in the Park"
(From the book *Caught Up in His Love*
by Leslie Y. Johnson, 1987.)

He beckons me from wherever I am
    To come to Him often
We meet in the park
    For here the harshness of the world
    Does soften.

I can better see Him
    In the grass, trees, and the lake
No better moments to flee the world
    And at His face a look to take.

His energy is ever full and free
    In all of nature it's so sweet
I loll about and talk to Him
    And leave my cares at His feet.

I certainly hate to leave the park
    But back into the world I must go
To live for and serve Him
    And forever His Spirit to show.

Lord, help us to remember that if we draw near to You, You will draw near to us, recalling also that you will never leave us nor forsake us.
    To You, O God, be all glory, honor, and praise!
    In Jesus' holy and precious name we pray.
    Amen.

8

Prayer for Salvation

(For the reader's study of God's Word, biblical references are inserted.)

Heavenly Father, Eternal God! Our Refuge and Deliverer! I praise You and give You thanks for giving us Your only begotten Son, that whoever believes on Him should not perish but have everlasting life (John 3:16).

Your Word tells us that if we confess Jesus as Lord and believe in our hearts that You raised Him from the dead, we shall be saved (Romans 10:9). For with the heart one believes unto righteousness; and with the mouth, confession is made unto salvation (Romans 10:10). Lord, give me a believing heart. Help my unbelief (Mark 9:24). For we are taught that we are saved by grace through faith (Ephesians 2:8). Thank You for Your saving grace.

Help me draw near to You, for then, as Your Word says, You will draw near to me (James 4:8). Enable me to resist Satan with Your Word so that he will flee (James 4:7). I repent of my sins and choose to follow Jesus as my Lord and Savior. May I come to know You, the only true God, and Jesus Christ whom You have sent, as this we are told is eternal life (John 17:30.)

To You, O God, be all glory, honor, and praise!

In Jesus' holy and precious name.

Amen.

Afterword

On December 31, 1968, my life, as I knew it, changed forever. Just past midnight, in a small modest home located at 19800 Monica in Detroit, Michigan, the Spirit of the Lord came upon me, overshadowing me with His power. This miraculous event regenerated me, which began a transformation in me: I no longer wanted the same life that I had previously led—a life focused on the world, rather than focused on the things of God.

Prior to this night, my meager time with God comprised a 60-second morning prayer, one-hour church service on Sunday morning, bedtime prayer, and a 30-minute Bible reading on Friday evenings from six to six-thirty. Soon after my encounter with the Spirit, I developed an insatiable appetite for something that I had witnessed only as a young girl in my grandmother's church— I began to yearn for God's anointing (His Presence) to fill my spirit. At this stage of my spiritual awakening, I only knew that when the Spirit came upon me, things in my life worked better for me. Yes, I had trials and persecutions, but the Spirit of the Lord in me and upon me caused everything to work for my good, even better than I could have imagined.

Now more than fifty years have passed since my first encounter with the Holy Spirit. Through the years, I have become attentive to God's Spirit leading and guiding me. I thank Him for being patient with me and nudging me back to the right path. When I can only cry and groan over my pains and sorrows, the Holy Spirit intercedes, advocates, comforts, counsels, helps, sustains, and stands by me. He has been with me through a divorce and single-parenting, which included major health issues with my children and myself. For instance, one September I needed a minor surgical procedure, but at the time, I was between jobs and without medical insurance. The Lord placed on my mind the name of a specific doctor who performed the procedure in his office and requested no payment. I knew that this was God's doing, and it was marvelous in my sight. In addition, the Lord has kept me alive for fifteen years with chronic leukemia that is now in remission.

Being betrothed to God through Jesus Christ is and has been my saving grace. The Lord called, invited, and welcomed me into an intimate relationship whereby I became His "betrothed"—He is my Bridegroom and I am His Bride (as one with the Church). The Lord is no respecter of persons. This invitation is open to all who believe in Him and receive His Son, Jesus Christ, as Lord and Savior. God so loved the world that He gave His only begotten Son to save the whole world. Acceptance of this call invites us into His grace, a life of favor with Him, doing and enjoying life His way. God Most High is King of kings, Lord of lords, and God of gods; and He desires that we commit our lives to Him—loving Him and keeping Him first in our lives. He wants to have an intimate, personal relationship with us. He is our Heavenly Father, Creator of the universe, Lord of hosts! God is love, and He has more than enough love for us all. The Bible tells us that He is good to all, and His tender mercies are over all His works (see Psalm 145:9).

So today, I ask you, "What is your pleasure?"—

—To go your own way, ignoring and rejecting God?

—To go the world's way Monday-Saturday, spending an hour or so with God only on Sunday? Or

—To go full-time in devotion to God, including Him in every area and decision of your life, making and keeping Him as your number one priority, keeping him first in your life for all times?

Are you willing to commit, pledge, promise your life to the Lord? The Bible tells us that He longs to "betroth" us to Himself in righteousness and justice, in lovingkindness, mercy, and faithfulness. Begin to seek Him through His Word; for God is His Word (see John1:1).

Will you accept a life as His betrothed? I have found that growing in a personal relationship with God has been the best decision of my life.

Printed in the USA
CPSIA information can be obtained
at www.ICGtesting.com
LVHW021317071023
760212LV00016B/731